Miracles Still Happen!

Devotional Journal

You Shall Have what you Decree!

Miracles Still Happen
by
Diana Etheridge

Copyright 2020 ICHAMPION Publishing

Published by iCHAMPION Publishing
P.O. Box 2352 Frisco, TX 75034
Content edit by Nikia Hammonds-Blakely and iCHAMPION Publishing
Library of Congress Cataloging in Publication Data Publisher and Printing
by iCHAMPION Publishing
Text Written By: Lady Diana Etheridge
Illustrated By: iCHAMPION Publishing
Cover Design By: Renee Huffman
ISBN: 978-1-7349212-6-7

Categories:
BIBLE
COMMENTARIES
RELIGION
Unless otherwise noted, all Scripture quotations are from the New International Version of the Bible. Copyright 1979,1980 & 1982 by Thomas Nelson, Inc., publishers.

Inspiration

A divine influence directly and immediately exerted upon the mind or Soul.

Everyone needs someone in their life that from time to time brings Inspiration into their life. When I met First Lady Diana, she greatly inspired my life. This book will greatly influence your life each time you turn the page. Life is a journey and each storm requires great Inspiration, pick up this book and see the change take place. After twenty-three years of marriage and twenty-four years of dating I can say my life has been inspired.

Bishop R. L. Etheridge II

Thank you

First, I would like to thank my Lord and Savior Jesus Christ for giving me a second chance at life to tell of his goodness and that He still perform miracles. Secondly, I would like to appreciate my husband Bishop Robert L. Etheridge II, for being my covenant partner, my rock, my spokesperson, and my encourager. He spoke over my life when the doctors gave up on me, I love and appreciate you. To my Family, Church Family, Extended Family and Friends who prayed for me while I was on my journey to recovery. I honestly believe that prayer changes things.

It was the Lord who allowed me to see how many of his people needing to be reassured that He is still a Miracle worker, a Prayer Answering God, and a Promise Keeper. I was told by God to Remind the people to Speak life over themselves even when they felt like giving up. Therefore, it is my prayer that whoever read these daily affirmations, will be Encouraged to keep the Faith and Remain Steadfast trusting that the Lord will see you through every storm or trial you may encounter.

(Matthew 9:29 NLT) says, then he touched their eyes and said, *"According to your Faith IT will Happen".*

Just do it

(Matthew 19:26) says, **that with God All Things are Possible.**

What is it that has caused your trust in God to waiver?

_____

_____

_____

_____

_____

_____

_____

_____

_____

_____

_____

_____

_____

_____

_____

_____

_____

_____

_____

_____

_____

_____

_____

"This is the Time to Put your Faith into Action, Just Do It!

What is God Saying?

(James 1:19) says, **My dear brothers, and sisters: everyone should be quick to LISTEN, slow to speak, and slow to grow angry.**

What is keeping you from hearing the voice of God?

_____

_____

_____

_____

_____

_____

_____

_____

_____

_____

_____

_____

_____

_____

_____

_____

_____

_____

_____

_____

_____

_____

"In This season, don't be so quick to speak; you might miss what God is saying"

Stay Strong

(Ephesians 6:10) tells us, **Finally, be strong In the Lord and in the power of his might.**

When you are feeling weak in your spirit, what do you pray to God for?

_____

_____

_____

_____

_____

_____

_____

_____

_____

_____

_____

_____

_____

_____

_____

_____

_____

_____

"Woman of God, the strength that God gives, can never be taken away; so, Stay Strong!"

What's Hindering You?

(Mark 11:24) tells us, **therefore I tell you, Whatever, you ask for in Prayer, believe that You Have Received IT, and it will Be yours.**

What's Hindering you?

_____

_____

_____

_____

_____

_____

_____

_____

_____

_____

_____

_____

_____

_____

_____

_____

_____

_____

"Believe and It will be Yours!"

(Psalms 91:11) says, **For He shall give His Angels Charge over you, to keep you in all your ways.**

Do you Pray and ask God to Keep you Covered?

_____
_____
_____
_____
_____
_____
_____
_____
_____
_____
_____
_____
_____
_____
_____
_____
_____
_____
_____
_____
_____

"*No matter what you May Face today,
Remember, God's Got You Covered!*"

God has a Promise & a Plan

(Isaiah 14:27) says, **Nothing, can stop God's plan for your life.**

Why is it hard to carry out the Plans that God gave you?

_____
_____
_____
_____
_____
_____
_____
_____
_____
_____
_____
_____
_____
_____
_____
_____
_____
_____
_____
_____

"God has a Promise & A Plan!"

Loose It & Let it Go

(Matthew 18:18) says, **Truly I say to you, whatever you Shall bind on Earth Shall be Bound in Heaven: and Whatever you Shall Loose on Earth Shall Be Loosed in Heaven.**

What are some of the struggles you have with speaking over Yourself?

_____

_____

_____

_____

_____

_____

_____

_____

_____

_____

_____

_____

_____

_____

_____

_____

_____

_____

_____

"Whatever you want, Speak It out of your mouth"

Keep a Praise on Your Lips

(Psalms 34:1) says, **I Will Bless the Lord at All Times; His Praise Shall Continually Be in My Mouth.**

What did God do that keeps a Praise on your Lips?

_____
_____
_____
_____
_____
_____
_____
_____
_____
_____
_____
_____
_____
_____
_____
_____
_____
_____
_____
_____
_____
_____

"No matter the trial or the test, keep a Praise on Your Lips"

Keep the Faith

(James 2:14) says, **Faith Without Works is Dead.**

What do you do when your Faith is being Tested?

_____

_____

_____

_____

_____

_____

_____

_____

_____

_____

_____

_____

_____

_____

_____

_____

_____

_____

_____

_____

"Keep your head up and Don't lose Faith"

God will Never Forsake You

(Hebrews13:5) says, **let your conversation be without Covetousness; and be content with such things as ye have; for I will Never Leave You, nor Forsake you.**

Are you content with what the Lord has given you, knowing that he will never leave you nor forsake you? Did Prayer do it, explain.

_____

_____

_____

_____

_____

_____

_____

_____

_____

_____

_____

_____

_____

_____

_____

_____

_____

"God will never Forsake You"

You are an Overcomer

(Romans 8:31) says, **If God Is for You, Who Can Be Against You.**

When people walked away from you, the Lord was by your side,
so why are you Thankful?

_____
_____
_____
_____
_____
_____
_____
_____
_____
_____
_____
_____
_____
_____
_____
_____
_____
_____
_____
_____
_____
_____
_____

*"Remember, you were born to be an overcomer,
Declare It Today"*

Abide in His Safety

(Psalms 91:1) says, **He That Dwelleth in the Secret Place of the Most-High shall abide under the Shadow of the Almighty.**

What stops you from communicating with the Lord?

_____
_____
_____
_____
_____
_____
_____
_____
_____
_____
_____
_____
_____
_____
_____
_____
_____
_____
_____
_____
_____
_____

"Don't let the enemy trick you, Abide in His Safety"

Walk in Peace

(Psalms 29:11) says, **The Lord gives Strength to His People; the Lord Blesses his People with Peace.**

What do you do when your peace is interrupted by the enemy?

_____
_____
_____
_____
_____
_____
_____
_____
_____
_____
_____
_____
_____
_____
_____
_____
_____
_____
_____

"Lean on God and walk in Peace".

Replace your Fear

(Zephaniah 3:17) says, **with his love, he will calm all of your Fears.**

What do you do when the Spirit of Fear tries to overtake you?

_____

_____

_____

_____

_____

_____

_____

_____

_____

_____

_____

_____

_____

_____

_____

_____

_____

_____

_____

"God's Love will replace Fear"

Stay the Course

(Psalms 119:105) says, **thy word is a lamp unto my Feet, and a Light unto My Path.**

How is the word of God a light unto your path?

_____

_____

_____

_____

_____

_____

_____

_____

_____

_____

_____

_____

_____

_____

_____

_____

_____

_____

_____

_____

_____

_____

"I encourage you to Stay the Course"

Do not Doubt

(Number 23:19) says, **God is not a man, that he should lie, nor a son of man that he should repent, has he said it will he not Do it, or has he spoke it; will he not make It good.**

Are you struggling with believing what God said he would do for you? why.

_____

_____

_____

_____

_____

_____

_____

_____

_____

_____

_____

_____

_____

_____

_____

_____

_____

_____

"Believe, Trust and do not Doubt"

Keep Pushing Forward

(2 Corinthians 2:14) says, **now thanks be to God, who always leads us to Triumph in Christ, and through us diffuses the Fragrance of His knowledge in every Place.**

What are you doing to prepare for what God has promised you?

_____

_____

_____

_____

_____

_____

_____

_____

_____

_____

_____

_____

_____

_____

_____

_____

_____

_____

"Keep Pushing Forward"

God will Rescue You

(Psalms 34:19) says, **the righteous person faces many troubles, but the Lord comes to the Rescue each time.**

How many times has the Lord come to your Rescue?

_____

_____

_____

_____

_____

_____

_____

_____

_____

_____

_____

_____

_____

_____

_____

_____

_____

_____

_____

_____

_____

_____

"God will bring you out, so stop Doubting him"

God will Rescue You

(Psalms 34:19) says, **the righteous person faces many troubles, but the Lord comes to the Rescue each time.**

How many times has the Lord come to your Rescue?

_____

_____

_____

_____

_____

_____

_____

_____

_____

_____

_____

_____

_____

_____

_____

_____

_____

_____

_____

_____

_____

"God will bring you out, so stop Doubting him"

Tame Your Tongue

(Proverbs 18:21) says, **Life and Death are in the Power of the Tongue.**

Our tongue can build others up or tear them down, who have you spoke life into?

_____

_____

_____

_____

_____

_____

_____

_____

_____

_____

_____

_____

_____

_____

_____

_____

_____

_____

_____

_____

"Speak Life in every situation"

God will Fight for You

(Psalms 24:8) says, **who is the King of Glory, the Lord God Strong and Mighty, the Lord Mighty in Battle?**

List some of the things that the Lord protected you from.

_____

_____

_____

_____

_____

_____

_____

_____

_____

_____

_____

_____

_____

_____

_____

_____

_____

_____

_____

_____

_____

_____

_____

_____

_____

"Remember, God will Fight for You if You Let Him"

Ask in His Name

(John 14:13) says, **whatever you ask in my name, this I will do, that the Father may be glorified in the Son.**

What are some of the things you are believing God for?

_____

_____

_____

_____

_____

_____

_____

_____

_____

_____

_____

_____

_____

_____

_____

_____

_____

_____

_____

_____

_____

_____

_____

_____

_____

_____

"Just Ask Him"

Seek God

(Matthew 6:33) says, **seek ye first the kingdom of God and his righteousness; and all these things will be added to You.**

What are you pursuing God for and what outcome are you expecting to get in return?

_____

_____

_____

_____

_____

_____

_____

_____

_____

_____

_____

_____

_____

_____

_____

_____

_____

_____

"Seek God in everything you Do"

Be Doers, Not Just Hearers

(James 1:22) says, **but be doers of the word, and not just hearers only, deceiving yourselves.**

Tell of a Time when you were led to encourage someone while you were going through yourself?

_____
_____
_____
_____
_____
_____
_____
_____
_____
_____
_____
_____
_____
_____
_____
_____
_____
_____
_____
_____

You are A mouthpiece for God, so lead by Example"

Pray Without Ceasing

(I Thessalonians 5:16-18) says, **rejoice always, pray without ceasing, give thanks in all circumstances; for this is the will of God in Christ Jesus for you.**

How do you Pray and Praise God when your facing multiply storms, list what it was that got you through?

_____

_____

_____

_____

_____

_____

_____

_____

_____

_____

_____

_____

_____

_____

_____

_____

_____

_____

_____

_____

_____

"In all things Pray, Praise God and believe that your breakthrough is Coming"

Seek God First

(Proverbs 3:5-6) says, **Trust in the Lord with All your Heart and lean not into your own understanding, in All thy Ways Acknowledge Him and He shall Direct your Paths.**

Tell of a time where you had to trust God and not yourself or people?

_____

_____

_____

_____

_____

_____

_____

_____

_____

_____

_____

_____

_____

_____

_____

_____

_____

_____

_____

"This is not the time to make hasty decisions; Seek God First!"

Pray & Believe

(Matthew 7:8) says, **For Everyone that asks Receives; and he that seeks find; and to him that knocks it shall be Opened.**

What are you asking God for when you Pray?

_____

_____

_____

_____

_____

_____

_____

_____

_____

_____

_____

_____

_____

_____

_____

_____

_____

_____

_____

_____

_____

"Pray and believe that he will Do It"

God is Listening

(Psalms 34:17) says, **The Righteous cry, and the Lord hear, and delivers them out of all their troubles.**

When was the last time you cried out to the Lord, and what did he say to you?

_____

_____

_____

_____

_____

_____

_____

_____

_____

_____

_____

_____

_____

_____

_____

_____

_____

_____

_____

"God is listening, and he is Moving"

Don't Lose Faith

(Romans 10:17) says, **now faith comes from hearing, and hearing the word of God.**

What are some of the things the enemy try to do to cause your faith to be shaken?

_____

_____

_____

_____

_____

_____

_____

_____

_____

_____

_____

_____

_____

_____

_____

_____

_____

_____

_____

_____

"Don't Lose Faith, your Blessing is coming"

Change is Coming

(Isaiah 40:31) says, **they that wait on the Lord shall renew their strength, they shall mount up with wings like eagles.**

Tell of a time where you had to wait for God's answer, and it seemed like it wasn't coming.
What did you do in your waiting season?

_____

_____

_____

_____

_____

_____

_____

_____

_____

_____

_____

_____

_____

_____

_____

_____

_____

"Be encourage, your change Is Coming"

Believe for a Miracle

(I Peter 5:10) says, **out of difficulties grow Miracles.**

What Miracles are you believing God for? List them.

_____

_____

_____

_____

_____

_____

_____

_____

_____

_____

_____

_____

_____

_____

_____

_____

_____

_____

_____

_____

_____

_____

_____

"Believe, your Miracle is on the way"

You Have Favor

(Psalms 5:12) say, **I am surrounded by God's favor.**

When God showed you favor, did it increase your Faith and Why?

_____
_____
_____
_____
_____
_____
_____
_____
_____
_____
_____
_____
_____
_____
_____
_____
_____
_____
_____
_____

"Be thankful for the Favor of God is on you"

(I John 5:14) says, **this is the confidence we have in approaching God: that if we ask anything according to his will, he hears us.**

What stops you from asking God for what you need and Why?

_____

_____

_____

_____

_____

_____

_____

_____

_____

_____

_____

_____

_____

_____

_____

_____

_____

_____

_____

_____

_____

_____

_____

"*All It Takes is Prayer and Faith*"

Put a Praise On it

(Psalms 150:6) says, **Let Everything that Has Breath Praise the Lord.**

Tell of a time where Praising God got you through, while in your waiting period?

_____

_____

_____

_____

_____

_____

_____

_____

_____

_____

_____

_____

_____

_____

_____

_____

_____

_____

_____

"Just put a Praise on It"

Look to the Lord

(I Chronicles 16:11) says, **look to the Lord and his strength; seek his Face always.**

What struggles have you faced while seeking God for your Healing, and how did you get through it?

_____

_____

_____

_____

_____

_____

_____

_____

_____

_____

_____

_____

_____

_____

_____

_____

_____

_____

"The Lord Heard You, so look to the him for instructions"

Stay Committed

(Proverbs 16:3) says, **commit to the Lord whatever you do, and he will establish your plans.**

What plans have you put before God and How do you intend to carry them out?

_____

_____

_____

_____

_____

_____

_____

_____

_____

_____

_____

_____

_____

_____

_____

_____

_____

_____

_____

_____

"No Matter what the Enemy Try to Tell You, "Do Not Listen" Stay Committed to God!

Stay the Course

(Matthew 5:44) says, **But I tell you, love your enemies and pray for those who persecute you.**

Tell of a time where you were instructed by God to pray for someone who hurt you, and what did God give you for being obedient?

_____

_____

_____

_____

_____

_____

_____

_____

_____

_____

_____

_____

_____

_____

_____

_____

_____

"You have to pray, forgive, and stay the course"

Don't Stop Believing

(John 3:16) says, **for God so loved the world that he gave his only begotten son, that whosoever believeth in him should not perish, but have everlasting life.**

How many times did the enemy try to get you to stop believing in God, and what did you do to stay the focused?

_____
_____
_____
_____
_____
_____
_____
_____
_____
_____
_____
_____
_____
_____
_____
_____
_____
_____
_____
_____
_____
_____

"Don't Stop Believing. The Lord is with you"

Keep Your Heart Pure

(Psalms 19:14), **Let the words of my mouth, and the mediation of my heart, be acceptable in thy sight, O Lord my strength, and my redeemer.**

Tell of a time when you were about to speak out negative words and the Lord shut your mouth.

_____

_____

_____

_____

_____

_____

_____

_____

_____

_____

_____

_____

_____

_____

_____

_____

_____

_____

_____

_____

_____

"Be careful with what you speak out of your mouth, the power of life and death is in your tongue"

Keep a Grateful Heart

(Isaiah 25:1) says, **O Lord you Are My God, I will Exalt you and praise your name, for in perfect faithfulness you have done marvelous things planned long ago.**

What have you done to show God that your grateful for what he has done for you?

_____
_____
_____
_____
_____
_____
_____
_____
_____
_____
_____
_____
_____
_____
_____
_____
_____
_____
_____
_____

"Be Grateful and Thankful"

Don't Let 'Em Steal Your Praise

(Psalms 150:6) says, **let everything that has breath praise the Lord, praise the Lord.**

What weapon do you use when the enemy tries to steal your praise?

_____

_____
_____
_____
_____
_____
_____
_____
_____
_____
_____
_____
_____
_____
_____
_____
_____
_____
_____
_____

"No matter who comes against you, don't Let 'Em Steal your Praise"

Take Time to Remember

(Jeremiah 29:12) says, **then you will call on me and come and pray to me, and I will listen to you.**

Think about a time when you went to God in prayer and he responded to you, list them; to remember how good he is?

_____

_____

_____

_____

_____

_____

_____

_____

_____

_____

_____

_____

_____

_____

_____

_____

_____

_____

_____

_____

_____

_____

"Remember Who Blessed and Kept you"

God Will See You Through

(Isaiah 43:2) says, **when thou passest through the waters, I will be with thee; and through the rivers, they shall not overflow thee; when thou walkest through the fire, thou shalt not be burned; neither shall the flame kindle upon thee.**

Who do you know that has been there for you during your worst season of trials?

_____

_____

_____

_____

_____

_____

_____

_____

_____

_____

_____

_____

_____

_____

_____

_____

_____

_____

"You might be in a fiery trial now, but God will see you Through"

It's a New Day

(Revelation 21:5) says, **behold I make all things new.**

If you are still living in the past, make today a fresh start by listing what you are about to leave behind you?

_____

_____

_____

_____

_____

_____

_____

_____

_____

_____

_____

_____

_____

_____

_____

_____

_____

_____

_____

_____

_____

_____

_____

_____

_____

"This is a New Day with new possibilities"

Your Labor is Not in Vain

(I Corinthians 15:58.) **Therefore, my beloved brothers and sisters be steadfast, un-movable always abounding in the work of the Lord, knowing that in the Lord, your labor is not in vain.**

What have you been waiting patiently for?

_____

_____

_____

_____

_____

_____

_____

_____

_____

_____

_____

_____

_____

_____

_____

_____

_____

_____

_____

_____

"Don't Lose patience in the hour, for your reward is coming"

Decree It & See It

(Job 22:28) says, **thou shalt also decree a thing and it will be established unto thee: and the light shall shine upon thy ways.**

As a praying woman, what have you declared over your life Today?

_____

_____

_____

_____

_____

_____

_____

_____

_____

_____

_____

_____

_____

_____

_____

_____

_____

_____

_____

_____

_____

"Decree it & See It"

There's Greatness in You

(Ephesians 1:4) says, **for he chose us in him before the creation of the world to be holy and blameless in his sight. In Love.**

God did not create you to be average, so write down what inspires you to be Victorious?

_____

_____

_____

_____

_____

_____

_____

_____

_____

_____

_____

_____

_____

_____

_____

_____

_____

_____

_____

_____

_____

"If God See Greatness In You, Believe It"

You are Healed

(Isaiah 53:5) says, **but he was wounded for our transgressions, he was bruised for our iniquities; the chastisement of our peace was upon him; and with his stripes we are healed.**

When you are believing God for your healing, deliverance or breakthrough, what scriptures do you meditate on?

_____

_____

_____

_____

_____

_____

_____

_____

_____

_____

_____

_____

_____

_____

_____

_____

_____

_____

_____

_____

_____

"You are Healed by his Stripes"

Perfect Peace

(Philippians 4:6-7) says, **And the Peace of God which surpasses all understanding, will guard your heart and your thoughts in Christ Jesus.**

The Lord is a peace- keeper, who do you go to when your Peace has been disturbed?

_____

_____

_____

_____

_____

_____

_____

_____

_____

_____

_____

_____

_____

_____

_____

_____

_____

_____

_____

"Perfect peace shall Be yours"

Your Season is Changing

(Nehemiah 8:10.) **The joy of the Lord is your Strength.**

When the enemy tried to steal your Joy, what word did you
throw back at him?

_____

_____

_____

_____

_____

_____

_____

_____

_____

_____

_____

_____

_____

_____

_____

_____

_____

_____

_____

_____

_____

_____

_____

"Your Season is About to Change, Speak it"

Use Your Power

(Romans 8:11) says, **the same power that raised Jesus from the dead is inside of you.**

What kind of power do you have and what have you done with IT?

_____
_____
_____
_____
_____
_____
_____
_____
_____
_____
_____
_____
_____
_____
_____
_____
_____
_____
_____
_____

"God Gave you Power Use It"

Push for The Promise

(Hebrews 10:36) says, **you need to persevere so that when you have done the will of God, you will receive what he has promised.**

Do you know what the Lord's will is for your Life, write them down?

_____

_____

_____

_____

_____

_____

_____

_____

_____

_____

_____

_____

_____

_____

_____

_____

_____

_____

_____

"This is not the time to quit, push for the Promise"

God Has Not Forgot

(Psalms 119:114) says, **you are my hiding place and my shield; I hope in your word.**

How many times did the Lord put you in a spiritual bubble, while he was refining you? Talk about it.

_____

_____

_____

_____

_____

_____

_____

_____

_____

_____

_____

_____

_____

_____

_____

_____

_____

_____

_____

_____

_____

"God always blesses those who remain steadfast"

Yield Not to Temptation

(Matthew 26:41) says, **watch and pray, lest you enter, into temptation; The spirit is willing, but the flesh is weak.**

When the enemy send distractions to stop you from praying and resist from being tempted, how do you stay focused?

_____
_____
_____
_____
_____
_____
_____
_____
_____
_____
_____
_____
_____
_____
_____
_____
_____
_____
_____
_____

"Be God Led, Not Flesh Led"

Now Faith is...

(Hebrew 11:1) says, **now faith is the substance of things hoped for, the evidence of things not seen.**

Was there ever a time when you lost faith in God. why?

_____

_____

_____

_____

_____

_____

_____

_____

_____

_____

_____

_____

_____

_____

_____

_____

_____

_____

_____

_____

_____

"Believe God and it will come to Pass"

The Blessing in Purity

(Matthew 5:8) says, **blessed are the pure of heart for they shall see God.**

Someone who has a pure heart is reliable and trustworthy, who has God told you to cover in prayer?

_____

_____

_____

_____

_____

_____

_____

_____

_____

_____

_____

_____

_____

_____

_____

_____

_____

_____

"A Pure Heart is Honorable to God"

Watch God Do it

(Jeremiah 17:14.) **"Heal me O Lord, and I will be healed, save me and I will be saved, for you are the one I will Praise".**

How many times has God had to put you back together when your mind, body and spirit was broken? List them.

_____

_____

_____

_____

_____

_____

_____

_____

_____

_____

_____

_____

_____

_____

_____

_____

_____

_____

_____

"Watch God Do It, your miracle is coming"